TONGUES
Languages of the God Class

BRANDON CORNELIUS SR

References and Sources

Speaking in tongues. Wikipedia. https://en.wikipedia.org › wiki › Speaking_in_tongues

https://mikesignorelli.com/science-confirms-speaking-in-tongues/

https://sharon.soundoffaith.org/2012/05/01/did-you-know-speaking-in-tongues-can-improve-your-health/

DEDICATION

I dedicate this book to the Lord Jesus Christ, my Lord and King.

I also dedicate it to my beloved wife, Denise Cornelius, and our two sons, Deuce and Chai. To my mother, Faye Cornelius, and my entire natural family—I honor you.

To my GRC family, my spiritual oversight, my co-laborers in the gospel, my friends, and my spiritual sons and daughters—I am deeply grateful for your support.

Finally, to those who truly helped me, encouraged me, prophesied over me regarding this book, and played a role in bringing it to fruition—thank you from the bottom of my heart. I love you all!

Apostle Brandon Cornelius, Sr.

TONGUES

Languages of the God Class

TABLE OF CONTENTS

TONGUES: LANGUAGES OF THE GOD CLASS

INTRODUCTION

This book is a journey into the discovery of the Languages of the God Class: Tongues. We will dive into one of the greatest mysteries that has been released to those who believe in Christ Jesus. The unveiling of this mystery will unlock a desire to dive deeper into the presence of God, to travel in the worlds we have access to in the spirit and to uncover the unlimited discoveries in the Kingdom of God. I pray that after reading this book, that you will desire to pray in more Tongues than you have ever prayed before in your life.

While reading, you must be aware that there are voice coded mysteries in God that are only unlocked through voice activation. These supernatural mysteries are only decoded through the voice of our spirit man. The voice of our spirit man is the languages of Tongues. The Bible says in Colossians 2:10 (NKJV), "and you are complete in Him,". In other words, our spirit man is complete only in Him, Who is a spiritual being in a spiritual world. The spiritual world has spiritual languages.

If you have never spoken this spiritual language, I pray that as you dive into the chapters in this book, the words will become a reality to your being. I pray that you receive the baptism of the Holy Spirit with the evidence of speaking in otherworldly languages.

You will also discover that there is a PEACE in Tongues that comes from another world that we cannot get in this world. Tongues will produce mental peace, soulish peace, spiritual peace and peace for your natural body! Our souls are fragmented, broken, incomplete and in need of renewal. When your spirit man prays, your soul has no understanding because your soul cannot comprehend COMPLETE language. Therefore, when your spirit man prays, complete language prays out the complete and perfect will of God. The Lord bypasses incompletion to bring forth completion. This is your invitation to enter a realm of completion.

CHAPTER 1

ANCIENT TECHNOLOGY

Thus says the Lord,

"Stand by the roads and look; ask for the ancient paths,

Where the good way is; then walk in it, And you will find rest for your souls.

Jeremiah 6:16 AMP

The languages of God are supernatural artifacts that were lost because of the Fall of man.

"For the Son of Man has come to seek and save THAT which was lost."

Luke 19:10 KJV

It did not say WHO was lost, but it says, THAT, in which the WHO is included in the THAT. The THAT is included in all things that Adam lost. Acts 3:20-21 says that "Jesus Christ was preached to you before, in whom heaven must receive until the times of restoration of ALL things, which God has spoken by the mouth of all His holy prophets since the world began." Jesus, the Last Adam, is restoring ALL things that were LOST.

7

One of the things that was LOST because of the disobedience of the First Adam, was a restoring of the languages of God. Since Adam, male and female, had the languages of God imparted on the inside of them, they were able to communicate with the spirit world and the natural world. They were able to communicate with every kingdom.

The operation of the first Adam, before the fall, was also seen in the operations of the Last Adam. Adam had languages that communicated with not only the Godhead but also all of the following: angels, of course other humans, animals, plant and tree life, air, wind, water, fish of the sea, birds of the air, cattle, every creeping thing in the earth, and every living creature of the earth. Anything that came into their realm or their jurisdiction, they had the language or the tongue to communicate with it. At the fall, they lost every in-sync communication except the ability to communicate clearly with other humans. Instead of mankind being able to be in sync with how God thought, moved, and operated, and them being able to remain in a place of communication on the Lord's frequency, the Lord had to lower His communication frequency in order to communicate with a dead and fallen human spirit.

There became a language barrier between mankind and the Lord. Instead of Adam being able to communicate with the Lord in a consciousness of union, of closeness, and of love, the communication became full of fear and separation because of sin. God and Adam were no longer yoked together as companions. They were no longer moving and communicating with one Another at the same pace, speed and frequency. Adam lost their spiritual location with God. They were no longer walking with Him, but they were outside of Him and apart from Him. Even their communication with one another, male and female, was no longer the same.

The Lord genuinely trusted Adam with responsibilities and government on the earth just as God ruled in Heaven. Adam had a glory mind. Their intelligence was from the light of God. The light of God made them the highest intelligent beings on the earth. Their intelligence was like God's intelligence. They were charged with reproducing that type of brilliance and intelligence throughout the earth. They were in a consistent receiving mode of revelation, counsel, wisdom and knowledge directly from the Lord. They were human, supercomputers in the earth. They did not need technology; they were the technologies. They were functioning from 100% brain capacity. Their brains were filled with light and life. They had no failure of the brain which means that they had no decay in the brain.

Prior to sin, death was not even in operation for them. They were living from an immortal state of being. They were operating from total recall. They could recall everything that the Lord downloaded into them. They had an unflawed and unhindered memory. Untainted memories without any ounce of traumas. A perfect operating system in all of the systems of their bodies. They were supernatural geniuses to the highest degree. They had master ingenuity. They were co-creators and co-reproducers like God and with God and with one another. The Lord materialized everything that He spoke to, and they had the same supernatural ability to materialize what the earth needed. Let's look at this genius in operation:

'Out of the ground the Lord God formed every beast of the field and every bird of the air, and brought them to Adam to see what he would call them. And whatever Adam called each living creature, that was its name. So Adam gave names to all cattle, to the birds of the air, and to every beast of the field.

Genesis 2:19-20 NKJV

Adam gave names to every living creature that he communicated with. This was during the time when there was not any violence, murder, shedding of blood, fighting, nor were there any humans harming each other. This was a time of peace and love. In fact, even animals and humans lived in peace without any tension between one another. Adam was able to rule without opposition to the animals. Also, the animals, during this time, got along with one another.

Later, Jesus comes on the scene, and He is operating at this perfected intelligence because He was innocent, pure, blameless and without sin, just like the First Adam before the Fall. Jesus is walking the earth as the Brilliant Light of the Godhead. He is marked and distinguished by unusual intelligence from above. He is functioning as the Light of the World and an Influencer of influential people. There was no greater intelligence upon the earth than Jesus Himself. He came as a Man, to show us our potential. He has reproduced Himself in us, so that we too can operate at high intelligence. This is so that we can live as brilliant lights of this world.

When the Lord decided to put His light in us, He imparted His intelligence in us. This is also one of the reasons that the Lord gave us Tongues which are His languages. Tongues can also be defined as light languages that help to produce God intelligence. When we pray in the spirit, we pray at the speed of light, the speed of glory, and the speed of the spirit. We do not fully understand this, because it is our spirit man praying and not the carnal side of us.

The most intelligent language that we can speak is the supernatural language of the Holy Spirit. His languages are unintelligent to our natural intellect but edifying and intelligent to our spirits. Every time we speak in His languages, we start jogging our memories of what we knew within eternity. What we knew with God before we were placed within our mother's womb. Tongues are an ancient technology. They are ancient languages that create communication with the Ancient of Days.

The Bible says that when we pray in Tongues, our minds are unfruitful or without understanding. It is unfruitful to the realm of the intellect but edifying in the realm of God. We edify ourselves when we pray in Tongues, but where is it edifying? It is edifying in the spirit. We cannot separate edification from intelligence.

Tongues help to increase our spiritual intelligence. They will also increase our intelligence in the realm of truth. One of the aspects of the word *truth* means God's reality. Therefore, Tongues will open up our understanding, so that we can view things from God's perspective and His reality. Those who do not take the time to pray consistently in Tongues will eventually start viewing things from a dogmatic, religious and mixed perspective. I do not see anything recorded in the Bible where it said that Jesus spoke in Tongues, BUT I do know that He spoke in the languages of God. Whatever that looked like or sounded like when He spent time with His Father, I do not know, but He did have that intimate language with His Father. It is because of Him that we have the same thing.

My point with that is, the Pharisees, Sadducees, Scribes and Lawyers were all very intelligent men, and they knew the Law and the Prophets like the back of their hands, but they did not know the heart and the spirit behind the Law and the Prophets. They did not speak the languages of God, and they were very dogmatic, self righteous and had

12

many mixed perspectives. However, Jesus viewed everything from the perspective of grace, truth and the heart of His Father. When our spiritual intelligence starts to increase, then we start seeing our minds renew. As our minds renew, immediately you start seeing your natural life being impacted by intelligence from the spirit realm.

The purest and most intimate language that we can speak are the languages of God. Those languages, where Paul said, we do not communicate with men, but we communicate with God because only He can understand the meaning of what we are saying. Jesus imparted these languages so that we can unlock secret truths and hidden things which are not obvious and comprehensive to the natural realm nor natural men nor natural intellect, but they release very tangible, fruitful, and divine results. There are several technologies that the Lord uses to help us to renew our minds, and Tongues are one of those technologies. The prefix *re*, means to do something over again. Therefore, when we *re*-new our minds, it means that our minds were once NEW in the realm of eternity. It is because of our fallen condition that we lost memory of what we knew in another dimension and timeframe, but the renewal of the mind restores us back to the mind that we had with God in the BEFORE realm.

The Lord gave us languages that can help to tame the whole body. Our tongue without being tamed or trained will automatically speak earthly, sensual and/or demonic wisdom. Therefore, the Lord gave us Tongues of fire to help govern our speech with wisdom from above. The carnal tongue has the ability to negatively change and destroy the course, the path and the way that a human thinks or behaves. However, the languages of God can change the course, path, and the way of someone's thinking and behaving from being destroyed and impacted negatively, to the direction and course of Heaven's influence.

The Holy Spirit uses our spiritual languages to teach us spiritual things. Spiritual languages will also help us to interpret spiritual things. The Bible says that spiritual people according to 1 Corinthians 2:15, "judges all things." They have the ability to judge all things properly and they can give a proper assessment of all things from the perspective, mindset, and heart of the Holy Spirit. God's languages help us to be proper judges in the spirit and in the natural world. Not to judge from a perspective of self-righteousness nor condemnation but to properly and rightly discern things from God's righteous heart.

Tongues are investments in the spirit. When we develop a lifestyle of Tongues, we are investing time instead of wasting time. Even though it may seem like we have wasted time in the natural world by praying in Tongues, in the spirit realm, we have gained time. Since the spirit realm moves at an accelerated pace, ultimately the time that we gained in the spirit will buy back time for us in the natural world. Every mystery revealed becomes a supernatural key that we can apply to our situations within the dimension of natural time, will either accelerate our process or bring an immediate solution. Even though Tongues can confuse the mind, meaning at the same time the mind is without understanding as we pray in Tongues, they can sharpen the mind. Tongues can increase the mind's intelligence. Additionally, praying in Tongues is a stress reliever if we become disciplined to pray in them long enough. We must learn to pray until what overwhelms us decides to break. We must diligently exercise our Tongues of fire until the fire of God dissipates all stress, anxiety, and fear.

.

BRANDON CORNELIUS SR

CHAPTER 2
THE GOD CLASS

*6That which is **born of the flesh is flesh**, and that which is **born of the Spirit is spirit**.*

John 3:6 New King James Version

The word *IS* means present tense, which it also has a plural tense, which is the word BE. By placing the plural tense in the second part of the scripture, it would say, that which is born of Spirit, BE spirit. The word *BE* means to have the same connotation as or to equal in meaning. For example, when we say that God IS Love, it also means that God BE Love. The word BE also means to have identity with or to belong to the class of. Therefore, as born-again believers that are born of the Spirit, we ARE spirits. Our true identity is spirit. We are part of the spirit class or the God class. As New Creation sons, we are a species of Christ beings that have been reproduced after God's own kind.

Make this declaration after me:

"I am a God-being. I am a God-species. I am a Godkind, and I am in the God-class."

You are not God Himself, but you are a species of being that have been born of, designed and recreated to be a part of His kind, in His class, a part of His species, and a part of His being. We are His OFFSPRING. We are carriers of His nature, His image, His likeness and His character.

The Word became flesh and dwelt among us, and we beheld His glory, the glory as of the only begotten of the Father, full of grace and truth.

John 1:14 NKJV

The word *begotten* is the Greek word *Monogenesis*, also where we get the word *Monogene*, which means Jesus has the DNA of His Father. He is the Only One of His Father's class or His Kind. Additionally, He was the Only Unique One and He was the Only Super Gene of His Father. This is what we have been born into. We have been born into the same super genes and now we are unique sons of our Father's kind. There are no other species that carry the same genes and genetics as the church of the Living God.

You have been regenerated (born again), not from a mortal origin (seed, sperm), but from one that is immortal by the ever living and lasting Word of God.

1 Peter 1:12 AMPC

The word *regenerated* here means to be born from above, but it also deals with, to become placed within the Monogenesis. Monogenesis is our Original Genesis. We have not been born from mortal origin, but our origin is from an immortal origin. The word *origin* means source or beginning. Therefore, we have been born out of an immortal source and an immortal beginning.

But as many as received Him, to them He gave the right to become children of God, to those who believe in His name: who were born, not of blood, nor of the will of the flesh, nor of the will of man, but of God.

John 1:12-13 NKJV

They did not become God's children by natural means, that is, by being born as the children of a human father: God Himself was their Father.

John 1:13 GNT

We have been born into a bloodline that is not of a natural bloodline. In fact, we have been born into a spiritual, divine bloodline. The same bloodline as Jesus Himself, who is the same Glorified Being that presently sits on the throne in Heaven. In 1 John, it says that "As He IS[PRESENTLY], so are WE {THE BODY OF CHRIST], in this world." We are in the world, but our origin is not from the world. Our origin is from ABOVE. Now, we are learning how to live from the world where we were birthed from. Jesus Himself is not just a Person, but He is also a Location. He permitted us to enter Him as a New Location. In this New Location, He has granted us access to new genetic material.

He rewrote our genetic code. He gave us access to new genetic information and made us genetic replicas of Himself, as Our Prototype. Jesus is the Prototype of a New Genetic species of being that are supernatural in nature. This species are now carriers of classified, otherworldly information. This species is the born-again believer in Christ Jesus. With that being said, we have inherited a spiritually, divine lineage through the bloodline of Christ

Himself. We were not born from the will of the flesh. We were not born from carnal and lustful desires. We were not born from sexual intercourse nor any other natural means of birthing children. We were not born from human beings. We were birthed from the matrix of the Holy Spirit and God Himself is our Father. It is because of regeneration that we have been granted access into the worlds that were BEFORE the natural world was even created.

When the WORD became flesh, He left a higher glory to take on the form of a lesser glory. Jesus became flesh so that He can bring flesh back into the same glory of the WORD. He raised what He was in the flesh to be reversed into the rank of spirits again.

For God so loved the world that He gave His only begotten Son
John 3:16 NKJV

Sonship is the only solution to the chaos of the world. Notice that the Father did not send a father, but the Father sent a Son. One of the meanings of the word *Father* means Source and a Son is the Reproducer of the Source. Hebrews says, that in the last days that God speaks to us by His Son, in Whom, the Father has appointed Him heir of ALL THINGS and through the Son, He made the worlds. Since it was through His Son that He made the worlds, it was only right to send His Son, to be the Solution to the same world that His Son created.

TONGUES: LANGUAGES OF THE GOD CLASS

The worlds that were created by the Son will only respond to the voice of sonship. Sonship language is the only language that the Lord is using to bring authentic order in the earth. Tongues are another form of sonship languages that the Lord uses to download fresh information from the New Location that we are in, into His sons, so that we can become the supernatural solutionists that we were always recreated to be. This is why in Romans 8; sons are the ones that are prophesied to help bring freedom to creation through the partnership of sons and the Holy Spirit. As we cultivate the oneness that we have with the Holy Spirit, through intimacy and obedience, we will start seeing gradual and at times, accelerated changes within the earth. We are His supernatural change agents.

And the glory which You gave Me I have given them, that they may be ONE just as We are ONE,

John 17:22 NKJV

As sons that share the same inheritance with Jesus Himself, when Jesus gave us His glory, He gave us inheritance from another world. We have inherited the same glory that Jesus received from His Father, so that we could qualify for oneness. The inherited glory of God made us one spirit with the Godhead and this same glory also gave us oneness with the entire body of Christ, not just the body that reside in the earth, but also the ones with His same DNA in Heaven.

*"In the beginning was the **Word**, and the **Word** was with God, and the **Word** was God."*

John 1:1 NKJV

The *Word* in the Beginning was Jesus and that same *Word* in Greek

is the word *Logos*. Logos means Blueprint. Therefore, Jesus is the Original

Blueprint of everything created. Jesus is God's DNA.

"And Jesus said to him, "Most assuredly, I say to you, hereafter you shall see heaven open, and the angels of God ascending and descending upon the Son of Man.""

John 1:51 NKJV

*Then Jacob dreamed, and behold, a **ladder** was set up on the earth, and its top reached to heaven; and there the angels of God were ascending and descending on it.*

Genesis 28:12 NKJV

The structure of DNA can be likened to a twisted ladder. In fact,

DNA is the "blueprint" of life. What Jacob saw in vision form, Jesus became

the Embodiment of that Structure. Once, the Holy Spirit, which is the Spirit

of Jesus filled us, He filled us with the DNA of God. Once our DNA binds

together with God's DNA, it establishes us within a divine covenant as His

divine offsprings. The DNA of God in us is a bond of oneness between

Heaven and Earth inside of us. The DNA of Jesus opened up a portal within

us to live a new and living way. As born-again believers, born from Him, we

have been made the gates of Heaven in the Earth.

The book of Hebrews says that it was FITTING for Jesus to bring

many sons into the glory. The word *fitting* means that it was suitable for Him or that it was right for Him to bring many sons into the glory. That level of ascension brought us into the God class. Jesus had the right to bring us into His world. This ascension gave Him the right to bring us into His seat of authority, with Him. Now, we have the right to live the God life on the earth. We have the right to live His existence in the earth. With that being said, as the God class in the earth, sin no longer has dominion over us because we are no longer of sin's kind. Before our ascension into glory, sin corrupted us from possessing a God consciousness and made us sin conscious. It is through the blood transfusion of Christ's blood into our spirit man that we are just as sinless as the One Who knew no sin.

This pure state of consciousness or awareness has given us access to become God conscious or God aware. Now, we have the supernatural ability to live from an awareness of the consciousness of God, and a reality as if we never knew sin just as He never knew it. He became sin, so that we can KNOW His righteousness. We have inherited something that is greater than the ancient forefathers and elders of old. The elders walked with God but as New Creation sons, however, we have inherited UNION with Him. God is not just walking with us, but He is also walking IN us as we are His house in the earth. Even though, the elders of old walked with God, they still were walking with Him without the redemption of His blood. The redemption of His blood provided us the permanent forgiveness for our sins.

Forgiveness of our sins does not just mean that we are no longer guilty of crimes, punishments and offenses against God, but it means that we have been completely separated and cut off from the nature that caused us to sin. The nature of sin was completely eradicated by the atonement of Jesus's shed blood. This is also the beauty of repentance. Repentance turns us from the dimension of darkness to the dimension of light and it also turns us from the power of Satan to the power of God. It is by way of God's power that we are able to uphold His standards of righteousness in the earth, because we became what He is.

In Hebrew, to repent is the word *shoov*, which means to be taken captive. In ancient times, when they took you captive, it was to destroy your home, leaving you with nothing to return to so that you would become fully committed to your new life. In the Kingdom of God, our freedom comes when our old house is destroyed. The old house represents our old life and our old nature in the bloodline of the First Adam. When the old house is destroyed, there is nothing about the old life nor the old nature to return to, as we are completely and wholeheartedly invested in the new house and in the bloodline of Christ. *Shoov* also means to return home. Hence, repentance means to return home to where we come from. It means to return to our origin that was before the First Adam and before our mother's womb.

Repentance in Greek does not just mean to think differently or to change one's mind but it also means to go beyond the natural realm. It is to think beyond the natural way of thinking and the natural way of doing things. We have acclimated to earthly movements, earthly motions and earthly patterns because of sin, but the Lord is teaching us how to live and move from beyond what we are acclimated to, accustomed to and familiarized with. Since we are no longer EARTH BORN, then we are no longer EARTH BOUND. The laws of the earth can be overridden by the higher laws from the realm that we were reborn from. The Lord has brought us into *zoe* life, *perissos* life, and eternal life. The remedy for premature death is the blood of Jesus. He says in Proverbs that, in the way of righteousness is life and, in its pathway, there is no death.

The blood of Jesus has given us the way or the path of righteousness because we have been made righteous, and in that path or that course of life, there is no death. It is only life producing more life. The Lord desires to teach us how to live above the realm that desires to cut our life off prematurely. Eternal life is not just life after death, but eternal life is a lifestyle of intimacy with Jesus here and now while we are still in the land of the living. We are living from the eternal, while we are in the realm of time.

Zoe life is the life that Jesus has given to us according to His original intent for mankind. Zoe life is the supernatural life of God. The same quality

25

of life that God lives. It is the God-life. Jesus came to transfer *zoe* life to us. He came to transfer the divine life that has the ability to invade our physical life and our soulish life. The more the Zoe life invades us, the more of the life of Jesus we have, and we obtain the supernatural ability to duplicate. Zoe life empowers us to live our life according to the original blueprint of the Godhead's design. Zoe life is not a makeover, but it is a takeover. Before the fall, Adam lived from Zoe, which means that we were always designed to live from Zoe. The fall stole that dimension of life from mankind and Jesus came to restore it back to us. Authentic dominion on earth will only be remembered when we re-learn how to live from Zoe.

Perissos life is a life of abundance, a life of excess, a life of overflow, a life that surpasses the expected, a life that is extraordinary, an above the normal lifestyle that is without limits. The perissos life is a RADICAL life in God, from God, through God and with God. The word radical means to become very different from the usual or traditional, to be extreme, or to be revolutionary. The Lord Jesus gives us permission to live a RADICAL lifestyle through Him, as Our Archetype.

Smith Wigglesworth made a profound statement and said, "God never intended for His people to be ordinary or commonplace. His intentions were that they should be on fire for Him, conscious of His divine power and realizing the glory of the Cross that foreshadows the crown." He also said,

"God has privileged us in Christ Jesus to live above the ordinary human plane of life. Those who want to be ordinary and live on a lower plane can do so, but as for me, I will not." We must learn to live in the conscious reality that the power of the new life is greater than the false perceptions of the old life.

The power of the gospel is the power of LIFE. It is the power of God's goodness toward humanity. The gospel message is the message of TRANSFORMATION. Normal human living for the New Creation species is not even authentic. Jesus did not come to make a BETTER ME, but Jesus came to REPLACE ME with a brand-new life altogether. If we refuse to reform our views, our perspectives and our ways of thinking, then we will continue conforming to the patterns of human living that He is longing to break us free from. He is stripping off the old garments of decayed living and clothing us with fresh garments of divinity and incorruptible living. According to 1 Peter, the incorruptible seed of Christ has already been implanted into us. We must learn how to grow into it, understand it, and live from it. The church, the God class of Christ in the earth, was designed to defy all human limitations that the law of sin and death has placed upon us.

For the law of the Spirit of life in Christ Jesus has made me free from the law of sin and death

Romans 8:2 NKJV

Originally, man was never designed to die but because of sin, man started experiencing death and because of death, mankind was lowered to human living full of decay, corruption and death. However, Jesus came to restore to us His life again and to raise us back into the height of His standards and His ways of living. There are no barriers nor any restrictions to how much of God that we can walk in nor how much of God can walk in us.

According to 2 Peter, we are partakers or sharers of God's divine nature and then it says because of this divine nature, we have escaped the corruption, the moral decay and the rottenness that is in the world through the world's lust. Divine nature is *theios* in Greek and it means God-like nature. It is the nature of the Godhead. Anytime you talk about nature, it means something inherent, fundamental characteristics, or original condition. The word *nature* also deals with words like natural and native and deals with kind or class. In other words, because of His nature in us, the God life should be natural to us, we are natives of God and His world, we are the God kind, and we are the God class. We carry the same nature of the ever-increasing glory.

As the God class, we qualify for classified information from another world. To receive classified information, you must be of a certain class or of the same class in order to access the information that is hidden to anyone that is lower than that class. As the God class, we have fully separated and have fully broken away from the corruption of the world that had us in demonic bondage. The Lord came to give us greater than what we had in the First Adam. Adam was earthly and of the earth and Jesus is from Heaven and He is Heavenly. Jesus came to remove us from the earthly image of our old nature and engraft us into the image of the heavenly nature.

The Church, which are the God class beings in the earth, are Heavenly men and women that are sent as agents and conduits to bring the culture of Heaven into Earth. We are not here to escape to Heaven, but we are here to become ambassadors of Heaven and gateways that allow Heaven permission to invade Earth. The Seed of God in us keeps us from sinning. What Seed is in us? The same Seed in Genesis that was prophesied to crush the head of the serpent. The Seed of God on the Cross that crushed, subdued, conquered, defeated and overcame the authority of Satan completely. Satan's authority has been completely brought under subjection by Jesus, as the Seed, and that same Seed is in us, by way of inheritance.

We have the same legal rights to continue to exercise and put into practice that same subjection over Satan and his kingdom through the power of the Cross, His resurrection and His ascension. We exercise these legal rights by faith. The God class are no longer sinners, but we are beings of His glory. The Lord had to cleanse a species with the Blood of Himself so that

He could fill this same species with Himself. When He filled us with Himself, He also gave us languages from Himself. Languages that can communicate directly with Him, without demonic interventions.

Look at this example, when a kingdom goes to take over another kingdom and they conquer that kingdom, one of the first things that the ruling kingdom changes within the captured kingdom is their language. They teach them how to speak the same language as the ruling kingdom. This is the beginning phase of teaching them the culture of the ruling kingdom. In the kingdom of God, when the Holy Spirit fills us, the first thing that He does is gives us His language, because this is the beginning phase of His takeover. This is the beginning phase of changing our culture into His culture. The more we speak in His languages, the more of the mysteries of His World and culture are imparted into us, and we start to understand these downloads by the gateway of revelation.

The Lord Jesus is the One that baptizes us in the Holy Spirit. The word baptize in Greek is *baptismo*, which means to become submerged into, to become soaked into or to become pickled into. Therefore, Jesus pickles us into the Holy Spirit. Anytime you pickle something, you change the form of it from the inside out. The act of pickling is a process, but when Jesus pickled us into the Holy Spirit, He accelerated the process and made us one with Him. He transformed our spirit man to become compatible enough and comparable enough to come into union with Him. When we were baptized into the Holy Spirit, we were also baptized into the entire body of Christ and through this same baptism, the entire God class have been made to drink into one Spirit.

The Holy Spirit is God in Liquid Form, He is DRINKABLE. We were made to be drinkers of the Spirit. We were made to be infused into Him and submerged into Him until we become Someone totally different. Notice I capitalized the *S*, that is because that Someone is no longer us. That Someone is Him. We should become more and more of Him. As we drink of Him, we become Him; As we drink of Him, we are transformed by Him and into Him. As an overflow of our union with Him, He gives us languages that are in the same depth of His class. Now, we have the supernatural ability to speak class to Class, spirit to Spirit.

CHAPTER 3
OUR SPIRIT MAN

⁹Do not lie to one another, since you have put off the old man with his deeds, ¹⁰and have put on the new man who is renewed in knowledge according to the image of Him who created him, ¹¹where there is neither Greek nor Jew, circumcised nor uncircumcised, barbarian, Scythian, slave nor free, but Christ is all and in all.

Colossians 3:9-11 NKJV

The passage of scripture above defines our spirit man. It describes the difference between the spirit man that was dead and the spirit man that is alive and awakened by the glory of God. The old man was functional and operational, but it also was considered dead because it had been separated from the Presence and Life of God because of the fall of Adam. Every person on the planet has been sent to the planet with a spirit man. Every human being is a tri-fold species: Spirit, Soul, and Body. We are actually spirit beings that are housed within an earth suit called a body, and we possess a soul. When God breathed into Adam, He breathed into the body of Adam, a spirit and a soul at the same time. The new man is the spirit man that is quickened and made alive by the Present Possession of the Holy Spirit. God decided to live in man and awaken man to man's original reality and also to man's original world.

*⁸But there is a **spirit in man**,*

And the breath of the Almighty gives him understanding.

Job 32:8 NKJV

This new man, which is your spirit man alive and awakened by the reality of God's life was also made in the image of God. The Holy Spirit decided to join together with, merge into union with, and become one with your spirit man. Spirit was able to inhabit spirit. This is the place where the Holy Spirit speaks to us. He speaks to the spirit that is in man. Our spirit man has eyes to see what God is saying and doing, and our spirit man also has ears to hear what God is saying and doing. We also have other spiritual senses that give us the ability to communicate with God. We have spiritual taste, spiritual touch, spiritual smell, spiritual feelings, spiritual knowing, and spiritual movements. There are more senses in our spirit man, but this is not the book to discuss that.

*[11]For what man knows the things of a man except the **spirit of the man** which is in him?*

1 Corinthians 2:11a NKJV

Our life is an ongoing revelation. We are a direct reflection of Christ living inside of the realm called time. We are IN time, but we are not OF time. Time is NOT our master, but Christ is. Therefore, since Christ is Ruler over ALL and we are in Him, then what does not master us, we must learn how to master. Thus, for us to master time, we must learn to live in the realm with the One who does master time. As we learn to live in sync with Him, time becomes a servant to us. Even though our outward man[body] is perishing, our spirit man is being renewed daily.

Time brings decay to the body but if we learn how to consistently walk in the spirit, we have the ability to live from our spirit man, which is in union with the Holy Spirit. It can quicken, rejuvenate and impart measures of life to our human body. As New Creation[kainos] sons, we are not slaves to chronos or chronological times, but we have the ability to seize many moments, opportunities and invasions of Kairos timings. Kairos timings are timings where time becomes redeemed. Kairos timings are those moments where Heaven invades Earth. Those are the times where time is overridden by the supernatural workings of another world. Those moments are in the spirit, they are not in the flesh. With that being said, because you are a kainos being, you will never understand, nor know the reality of the authentic you, without Kairos.

Our spirit man is the real us, so he understands the real us, but our minds have to be renewed to the knowledge and the understanding that the spirit man has about us. This is where Tongues become a tool to help us to communicate beyond an unrenewed mentality. Tongues are our spirit man's communication. As the chapters go on, I will get into more depth about Tongues and our spirit man and the spirit world.

Our spirit man longs for Heavenly activity. Your flesh craves natural dimension activity. This is the constant war between which one will be lord. Whomever we consistently yield to will govern our lifestyles.

²⁷The spirit of a man is the lamp of the Lord

Proverbs 20:27a

Our spirit man is the lamp of the Lord. Another version says that it is the candle of the Lord. The same word in Hebrew is *neyr*, which means the burner. The spirit man is the burner of the Lord, or your spirit man is what burns before the Lord. Our spirit man is a fiery being, and a light being that was created after the Consuming Fire Himself. Your spirit man loves to burn because it was designed to burn. The burning of the Lord keeps our spirit man strengthened. The dimmer the fire, the weaker our spirit man becomes.

Our spirit man is a burning lampstand that burns with the Lord's fire. A living candlestick, a living menorah which is one who burns with the fire of the Seven Spirits of God. You are a mystery within a mystery. Just as you will forever be learning about Christ, you will forever be learning about yourself, because we shine as His reflections.

We are lights within darkness. Your spirit man is a heavenly place. It is a mobile ark that the Lord uses to lead, guide and govern us throughout life. When we fail to burn within our spirit man, we tend to gravitate toward an illegal lifestyle, that the Lord never planned out for us to live. A life that was never ordered nor ordained by Him. The Lord can redeem what we allow Him to redeem, but there are many paths that we can avoid by simply burning for Him and allowing the same God that led Israel by fire, to lead us by His inner fire.

The dimmer the inner flame, the more desensitized we become to His leadership, His voice, His activities, and His movements. It is because we inhabit the inner Presence of the Holy Spirit, that our spirit man is addicted to the Presence of God. This is why having a strong spirit that is blazing with the fire of God, can help us to overcome any addictions that try to become replacements for the functioning and the comfort of the Holy Spirit.

The power that pulls us strongly to natural, earthly and fleshly cravings and desires can be overpowered by the same power that raised Jesus from the dead. This power can give us a stronger craving for the Presence of God. When the Presence of God becomes your addiction, there is nothing on the earth that can bring any level of satisfaction for you. All other things become a lesser enjoyment. There are things that you will still enjoy but they will never take precedence over the Presence of God.

*[3] [The Father] has delivered and drawn us to Himself out of the control and the dominion of darkness and has **transferred** us into the kingdom of the Son of His love*

Colossians 1:13 Amplified Bible, Classic Edition

When you were regenerated and birthed from above, birthed from Heaven, and birthed out of the matrix of the Spirit, a spiritual transfer happened with your spirit man. You were translated from one dominion into another dominion. From the domain and dominion of Satan to the domain and dominion of King Jesus. Your spirit man was an agent of Satan and his domain until the payment of the Blood of Jesus made a transfer in the spirit realm. Now, you are an agent of God Himself.

Your allegiance and alignment are no longer under Satan's rule. Now, you are submitted under the government of Christ. You have been spiritually submerged into His body and engrafted into the Vine of Life. There is no separation in the spirit realm between you and Christ and you and Christ's body. We are all spiritually connected as ONE. The Dove of the Spirit has a resting place within the spiritual body of Christ.

The supernatural world always affects the natural world. The supernatural world is the governing influence over the natural world because the natural world came out of the supernatural world. With that being said, the spirit realm has influence over all of the following: our marriages, our money, our relationships, the way we think, the decisions that we make, our emotions, our movements, the way that we speak and behave, and the list goes on. Subsequently, if we are going to effectively live life in the natural world, then we need to learn how to engage properly with Heaven's supernatural world.

This is where your spirit man plays the biggest role. The spirit man partners with the Holy Spirit, so that He can learn the depths of what God has reserved in Heavenly realms. We are not just seated in Heavenly realms, but we must learn through the tutelage of the Holy Spirit, how to legislate from those same Heavenly realms.

> *[18]We know that whoever is **born of God** does not sin; but he who has been born of God **keeps himself,** and the wicked one does not **touch him.***
>
> *[19]We know that we are of God, and the whole world lies under **the sway of the wicked one.***
>
> *1 John 5:18-19 NKJV*

The reality of us being birthed out of God Himself, for us, was a change of location. This location is a hiding place. It is Him in us and us in Him. It is a place where the only time that the enemy can have an advantage over us is if we come out from within that place by making provision for the flesh. This location gives us higher visibility and a higher perspective to keep ourselves. We can see the enemy's temptation from a spiritual vantage point. When we are in the location of God, the hiding place of God, we have supernatural grace to keep ourselves. To keep ourselves means to protect ourselves, or to spiritually guard ourselves. The Lord gives us supernatural weapons and technologies to guard against the wicked one's touch. To touch here means to have influence upon. It also means to leave such an impression upon us that it alters or modifies us.

Many times, you can tell that he has altered us through our speech, conduct, way of thinking and lifestyles. A wicked touch can alter you and set you down a path of destruction. I thank God for His hiding place guardianship. The wicked one has much sway upon the natural dimension and those that are body ruled, carnal minded or governed by the sight realm of the natural dimension. The word *sway* means to be a controlling influence. The wicked one is a supernatural being that has controlling influence. This controlling influence is only over those that are either in his location or those that have removed themselves from the location of God's hiding place. Influence is always won in the spirit first. Therefore, if we want to learn how to gain greater influence over Satan's controlling influence, we need to remain hidden in Him. We must remain under the governance of the One, of Whom I live, I move, and I have my being.

Be transformed by the RENEWING OF THE MIND
Romans 12:2 NKJV

As spirit beings, our minds need to become renewed so that the transformation that has already taken place within our spirits can become not just an internal reality but also an external reality. The Greek word for transformed is *metamorphoo,* in which we get the English word metamorphosis, from this Greek origin. If you break down the words, you get *meta* and *morph*. These two separate words have powerful meanings. Meta means beyond and/or super and morph means to change forms. Therefore, the process of renewing our minds will start changing us into the form of super and beyond. We start becoming something different altogether. We start living in the reality of the world that already exists inside of us. The Kingdom world. God's world become the habitation that we live in. Again, the spirit realm is the more dominant realm. It is the realm that influences and governs the natural realm.

Our minds are more influenced by the spirit realm than we are even aware of. The Lord knows this, so He gives us the command, the charge, and the responsibility through Apostle Paul, to renew our minds through spiritual technologies. He knows that the greatest battles that we face are the battles of the mind and these battles are spiritually engineered. Hence, when the Lord commands us to renew our minds, the Lord is influencing us to think like spirit beings more than natural ones. If we are going to gain higher ground within this war between light and darkness, then we have to think within higher dimensions than the spirits that are diligent in trying to influence us to always think dark. Influence is always won in the spirit realm first. This is why Paul gave credence to us, as New Creation sons, to think Heavenly minded. He charges us to think on things that are above and not on the earth. Think in the realm where Christ is. Think about where we are seated in Heavenly places.

One of our spiritual technologies is Tongues and these Tongues will cause us to shift our focus from the natural realm into the spiritual realm. The renewing of our minds is a series upon a series of mind relocations. Those mind relocations bring transfiguration. The same way that Jesus transfigured on the mountain, is the same type of location change that we will come into conditionally, once our minds relocate. Our minds are supposed to fully shine with the light of His glory. One of the types of evidence of our minds being renewed is when the things of the spirit are becoming common sense. When that world and the operations of that world start to become just as natural as the natural world is to us.

For as many as are led by the Spirit of God, these are the sons of God
Romans 8:14

One of the aspects of the word "led" means to be influenced by or to be governed by. Thus, whenever our desires come under the government of what the Holy Spirit desires, then we start seeing the fruit of becoming led by the Spirit of God. Our desires can be either spiritually manipulated by demonic forces or spiritually inspired and moved by the Holy Spirit.

For the flesh lusts against the Spirit and the Spirit against the flesh; and these are contrary to one another, so that you do not do the things that you wish'

TONGUES: LANGUAGES OF THE GOD CLASS

Galatians 5:17

The Holy Spirit gives us spiritual lusts. It is a major distinction between the spirit of lust and spiritual lusts. The word *lusts* in its original connotation means strong desires. Which means that the Holy Spirit gives us strong desires for God and the things of the Kingdom. Your flesh does not desire God, the Kingdom nor Kingdom things, but your spirit man does because it is one with the Holy Spirit. The flesh has strong desires that oppose your spirit man, and the spirit man has strong desires that oppose the flesh. These two mindsets and desires are antagonistic to one another. They oppose one another, in order to govern us and lead us into the obedience of the spiritual entity that is doing the leading.

The proof of our desires is in what we pursue. Accordingly, whatever dimension that we consistently pursue, the desires of that dimension will become our dominant desires. The Holy Spirit is the Spirit that produces sonship. This is our adoption, birth, inheritance and our freedom. Our sonship is in the spirit not in the natural because God is Spirit. He gave birth to us and adopted us in the spirit. We have been legally made sons within the divine family of God. It is because of this reality, that we have the ability of sharing the same sinless reality and sinless lifestyle that Jesus lived and that He lives. We will never understand the life of sonship without the intelligence of the Holy Spirit.

CHAPTER 4
GATEWAY LANGUAGES

But you shall receive power when the Holy Spirit has come upon you; and you shall be witnesses to Me in Jerusalem, and in all Judea and Samaria, and to the end of the earth.

Acts 1:8 NKJV

When the Holy Spirit comes upon us, we shall receive power. The word come upon means when the Holy Spirit fills us or when He wears us like a garment. Therefore, the first evidence of a believer, one that has been raised into the God class, being filled with the Holy Spirit, is POWER from God. The Holy Spirit wears us like a glove and demonstrates His power through us. The sign of a continually filled believer is POWER.

And these signs will follow those who believe: in My name they will cast out demons; they will speak with new tongues; they will take up serpents; and if they drink anything deadly, it will by no means hurt them; they will lay hands on the sick and the sick will recover.

Mark 16:17-18 NKJV

All of these signs that Jesus just described, casting out demons, speaking with new Tongues, taking up serpents, no hurt coming to those that drink anything deadly, and laying hands on the sick and the sick recovering - are all demonstrations of POWER. Which also means that

45

Tongues are a part of the power package that comes with being filled with the Holy Spirit.

Think about this, all of these are demonstrations, in which all demonstrations need to be either seen or heard. Therefore, in order to demonstrate casting out demons, you need people that have demons; in order to take up serpents, you need serpents. For example, Paul was able to demonstrate this when he was bitten by a viper and he shook the viper off, but he did not die. That was a display or demonstration of the power we attain by being filled with the Holy Spirit. Also, in order to drink something deadly and it will not harm you, you would first need to drink something poisonous *(which I am not suggesting you do intentionally),* and in order to lay hands on the sick, you need sick people.

Notice that Tongues are the only demonstrations of power that do not include other people nor other things to become demonstrated. Whether you get baptized in the Holy Spirit in private or whether you get baptized around other people, Tongues are the initial evidence that you have just been filled with the Spirit. Tongues were demonstrations of the arrival of the New Covenant. They were proof that believers were baptized into the mystical body of Christ. According to 1 Corinthians 12, the Holy Spirit has baptized us into the body of Christ. He united us together as a spiritual body unto Jesus.

TONGUES: LANGUAGES OF THE GOD CLASS

At the Tower of Babel, men were trying to build a supernatural gateway into the heavens. They were trying to gain illegal access into the dimensions of God. In the upper room, the Holy Spirit is the Legal Gateway into the realms of God, so He became legal access back to God. At the tower of babel, the Lord came down and confused their languages and men no longer spoke one universal language, because their Tongues were divided in the earth. They no longer spoke the language of oneness. The Lord broke up the very thing that united them, it was their languages. However, at the upper room, the Lord restored a universal language of oneness in Him. He imparted into them divided languages that would unite people back into oneness. Now, through the reproduction of the baptism of the Spirit that took place in the upper room, as the body, we all have access to this same oneness language that the Lord originally intended for us to speak.

In a corporate setting, Tongues are diverse languages that have the supernatural ability to influence people into being on one accord. I truly believe that they knew the power of Tongues and they continued to repeat the pattern of praying together on one accord, with the technology of Tongues.

Tongues are drunken languages. In Acts 2, some of those that heard the believers in that day speak in Tongues were amazed but there was another group that mocked them for speaking in Tongues and said that they were full of new wine. Which meant that they thought that they were DRUNK. Peter, full of the Spirit, gave interpretation to the demonstration of what was on display. Peter actually admitted that they were all drunk, but they were not drunk in the natural dimension. They were drunk from the dimensions of God. They were displaying a realm of otherworldly drunkenness. We are drinkers of the new wine from the realm of God. The realm where being drunk in the Spirit is normal intoxication. The gift of getting drunk in the Spirit places us back in our right minds.

Anytime you are drunk on a substance, you become controlled by that substance. Natural drunkenness starts in the flesh, but I believe that there are demonic spirits that also influence our behavior. Therefore, when we get drunk in the Spirit, that condition or state of mind allows us to become controlled and influenced by the influence of the Holy Spirit.

When we take time to continually pray in the spirit, we create an avenue that the Lord uses to keep us drunk in the spirit and also to fill us back up with His Spirit. Ephesians 5:18 states, "do not get drunk with wine because that is debauchery, but be ever filled with the Holy Spirit." That means that becoming drunk on natural wine or natural alcoholic beverages is debauchery. Another word for debauchery is dissipation, which means that being drunk with natural wine will lead us into walking in the character of a person that is not born again.

The remedy to not walk in debauchery is to be continuously filled with the Spirit. The remedy to not having the need nor the desire to want to get drunk on natural wine or natural alcoholic beverages is to continuously be filled with the Spirit. When we pray in Tongues long enough, Tongues have the supernatural ability to rapture believers into an ecstatic state, where the believer will no longer be master's nor in control over their own reasons, nor their own consciousness. They gain another and a higher awareness. A trance-like ecstasy that will carry us out of and remove us from our normal state of function. The Holy Spirit will rapture us into the realm of the Lord. A place where revelations and visions start to become clear and normal. Believers, whom are not necessarily seers in the Spirit can start seeing in the Spirit when we are caught up in these realms. The act of praying in Tongues awakens all of our spiritual senses, but our spiritual sight and spiritual hearing become the main senses that are awakened.

Tongues are gateway languages that stir up the power of God in us. They also keep us in the power of God and build us up to operate in the His power. Tongues have the supernatural ability to stimulate us into greater activities of the Spirit. They stir up the gifts in us.

The Bible says that when the Spirit comes upon us, we become CLOTHED with power. The continual refilling of the Spirit will cause us to manifest spiritual garments of power. Every time we get filled with the Spirit, we put on a different garment of power in the spirit realm. When we become filled with the Spirit, the Spirit gives us power to overcome. Also, being filled with the spirit gives us power to push back fear. In addition, praying in Tongues for an extended period of time helps us to dismantle fears. One of the Hebraic meanings of the word power means the ability to control life. As we surrender control of our lives to Him and allow Him to continue filling us with His Spirit, we eventually learn how to control life His way. It is because of Him that we are supernatural beings and since we are supernatural beings, we have the ability to do things that ordinary people cannot do and handle things differently from how ordinary people handle them.

When we are not filled with the Spirit, we tend to handle things in life, as if we do not have a Helper. When we are not filled with His Spirit, we will become less and less compliant to His ways and we tend to do more complaining than overcoming. When we are not filled with His Spirit, we will eventually lack the power to overcome patterned struggles, patterned addictions and strong temptations. We tend to fall prey to these things, when we are not filled with the Spirit and strong enough in the Spirit. We are more sensitive to His leadership when our spirits are strong in Him. The strong desires of the flesh will always govern those that refuse to take up the diligence and the discipline to walk in the Spirit.

The word *walk* means to be aligned with, but it also means to converse with the One. This also means that walking in the Spirit is a continual conversation with God. The most efficient way to have a continual conversation with God is to pray in the languages of God. If I am conversing in the languages of God, my spirit is conversing with God. Conversing in the languages of God unto God will keep us walking in the Spirit. 1 Corinthians 14:14 states that if I "pray in tongues, my spirit prays but my understanding is unfruitful." In other words, when I am praying in Tongues, my spirit is praying but I do not understand what I am saying. My mind becomes useless, and it has no part in what my spirit is praying. My mind becomes unproductive when I am praying in Tongues. My mind cannot comprehend what I am saying and not even yield to what I am saying because it takes faith to pray from my spirit.

The Lord was very wise when He gave us Tongues. He gave us a supernatural technology that can build up faith for unseen realities but at the same time bypass our own unbelief and doubts. He set it up to where we can continually converse with Him, even in the midst of our busyness. Continuous conversing in the Spirit keeps us from fulfilling the desires of our flesh. If we start sensing our minds moving toward the desires, thoughts and feelings of the flesh, we need to start praying in the Spirit until those thoughts become removed. If we practice these things as a lifestyle, then we will start encountering more victories in areas where we saw more failures in. Continual conversing with God makes us more and more aware and sensitive to His nudges, promptings and the pushes of His Spirit in our everyday activities. This is the realm where we refuse to quench Him and refuse to grieve Him.

Tongues, for many, have become a lost art for a divine life. Again, the word Tongues means the word languages. When we pray in Tongues, we are praying in the languages of God. I wanted to give a brief reminder of this: Tongues are a supernatural technology that will help to acclimate us to the spirit world. Mystical beings speak in Tongues. If you speak in Tongues, you are a mystical being. There are mysteries about God and about yourself that you have the supernatural ability to pray out and discover when we pray in Tongues. Tongues were given for the sake of what Tongues produce. We speak in Tongues because they bring productivity in the spiritual dimension but will manifest and yield tangible rewards in our natural lives.

Tongues are gateway technologies into the God-life. In fact, because of the realm of mysteries, Tongues make us well-diggers in the spirit. Many times, we will dig wells in the spirit by praying in Tongues

NOW for what we will see manifestation of LATER. That means that praying in Tongues will help us to build a reserve for when a demand comes for that specific thing that we dug into, in the spirit. Our spirit man is a traveler, and he will communicate in the dimension that he has traveled to. Accordingly, when we are praying in Tongues, even though our mind does not comprehend, our spirit man starts to travel into different locations in the spirit and communicating with different beings in those locations. Our spirit man is multilingual in the spirit world, and he can also speak every language in the earth, when there is a need, prompted by the purposes of God. The Holy Spirit will escort your spirit man into different locations in the realm of the spirit and in the earth, with your awareness and without you being aware of it, especially as you give yourself over to praying in tongues for an extensive amount of time. Why? It is because your spirit man is not bound, governed by nor restricted by space, time, geography nor the laws of the natural realm. I will get into more of the locations of Tongues in the next chapter.

Tongues are also spiritual regulators. They tend to help bring adjustments to our internal conditions, which also turns into external adjustments. Those times when you notice yourself manifesting the character of the flesh, if you take the posture of praying in Tongues, you will start noticing those fleshly desires start to become weaker in you.

Continuous prayer in Tongues will shift our desire from carnal desires to kingdom desires.

Tongues are also destiny locators. There are portions of our destiny that we will fail to step into, if we do not pray in Tongues. Tongues help us to pray out destinies and they also help us to pray ourselves into destiny. In the kingdom, destiny is not just about destination, but destiny is also about coming into an IMAGE.

The book of Romans 8:29 states that "He has PREDESTINED us to be conformed into the IMAGE of His Son." Image deals with being a genetic replica of the One that you are replicating. Image also deals with becoming a reflection and it also deals with being shaped into the same character. Therefore, praying consistently in Tongues will start to shape our character, so that we become a reflection of God and thus a seen image of an unseen God. We can start living a life that says, if you see me, then you see Jesus. There are great men and women of the Spirit and of power, like John G. Lake, that have testified that the way to a greater and more effective ministry in the kingdom is when we take great amounts of time praying in Tongues. Tongues are a gateway into spiritual growth.

"He who speaks in a tongue edifies himself."
1 Corinthians 14:4 NKJV

54

TONGUES: LANGUAGES OF THE GOD CLASS

The word edifies is the word *oikodomeo* in Greek, which has several different meanings as you break down words and definitions. According to oikodomeo, when we pray in Tongues, we build up our spirit man and make him strong, promote our own spiritual growth, cause our character to develop and become mature, build spiritual stability, and instill boldness within ourselves. Here are more versions of that same scripture that I just spoke about.

"The one who speaks in tongues advances his own spiritual progress"
1 Corinthians 14:4 TPT
"A person who speaks in tongues is strengthened personally
1 Corinthians 14:4 NLT
"When a person speaks in another language, he helps himself grow"
1 Corinthians 14:4 GW

New Tongues are languages that have not been previously learned in our fallen state. The Greek word *Kainos* in "*Kainos* Tongues" or "*Kainos* languages" is the same word that is derived from New Creation, which refers to a "New" or Kainos species. New Creation believers speak in new Tongues. In other words, the Kainos species in the earth speak in Kainos languages. Tongues are languages that were not learned by being in the lineage of the first fallen man. Tongues are not fallen languages, but they are languages of the ascended.

There are languages of God that are the languages of the immortal. Languages where only God can understand. Also, Paul talks about speaking in the Tongues of angels. God and angels are both in the realms of immortality. Tongues will allow us to take spiritual blueprints laid out in DIVINITY and understand them in our HUMANITY.

Tongues are the divine languages of God that are proof that our High Priest lives forever. They are priesthood languages after the order of Melchizedek, and they were languages that manifested after the ascension of Jesus into His High Priest seat and royal throne. These languages became active after the sending of Another Helper and Comforter, the Holy Spirit. Jesus, who is the High Priest according to the legacy of Melchizedek, is now functioning from His heavenly administration. As He released the outpouring of His Spirit, He released with the outpouring, the technology of Tongues in order to help us administrate Heaven's agenda and culture.

Tongues are also proof that we carry new DNA and new genetics. On the Day of Pentecost, the Holy Spirit gave them an utterance and they began to speak. This speaks to the union or oneness between the Holy Spirit and our spirit man. Every union is purposed for partnership and Tongues are union languages. The word *utterance* means to speak out or to speak boldly under divine inspiration, therefore, Tongues are not for the quiet. Utterance also means to articulate sounds. These sounds are articulated supernaturally. In addition, utterance means that this speech was not common speech. This was dignified and elevated communication so what seems like babbling nonsense in one realm, is intelligent speech in another realm. You must never become ashamed of your intelligent speech from another realm.

CHAPTER 5
LOCATIONS

There are depths in the spirit realm that we will never reach without praying in Tongues. Likewise, there are depths where your understanding will not be reached unless you pray in your heavenly languages. When we pray in Tongues, we are hearing the voice of our spirit man. We need to immerse our life in Tongues. Many may say, we already pray in Tongues, but it is an intense difference between a person that prays in Tongues and a person who has a lifestyle of saturating themselves in Tongues. A person that saturates themselves in Tongues can walk and flow in the current of God's rivers and not simply experience momentary or temporary splashes.

There are dimensions of Tongues that will break us into the dimensions of the spirit where the Spirit of Revelation teaches. This means that you can saturate your life in Tongues so much that the Spirit of Revelation starts to take over. The Lord will cause us to start interpreting our own Tongues. Interpretations are downloads of revelation. This is where we start interpreting the languages of God. The Lord will start breaking us into a realm of abundant downloads.

The lack of knowledge happens because people refuse to gain the knowledge, but a lack of knowledge also happens because there are realms of revelation that are locked up from the lazy, those that lack discipline and the non-seekers. In the garden, they [Adam] heard the sound of God coming as a wind during the day. Similarly, in the upper room, they heard God coming as a wind on the DAY of Pentecost. There was a SOUND in the garden and there was a SOUND in the upper room. Within both SOUNDS, God was talking. In the garden, God was talking outwardly TO man. In the upper room, God was talking inwardly THROUGH man. In the upper room, God came from Heaven to restore that same intimacy and fellowship with man that He had with Adam before the fall. In the garden, it was fellowship through visitation but in the upper room it became fellowship through habitation; God came to fill man so that He can live in man.

Just as the Lord filled them in the upper room with His languages, the Lord had also filled Adam with His language. When Adam spoke, they were speaking the languages of God. From Genesis 1 to Genesis 11, we see that there was only one universal language spoken by man. From Adam all the way to the Tower of Babel. In the time of the Tower of Babel, they were building an illegal gateway to Heaven, and the Lord came down and confused the language of men to bring division among them and division within their languages.

TONGUES: LANGUAGES OF THE GOD CLASS

In the Book of Acts, the Holy Spirit, which is the Legal Gate of Heaven, came and gave the languages of Heaven, languages that would unite men, so that men would speak the same languages of God again. In the garden, God came from Heaven to enjoy intimacy and fellowship with man. The garden was the fruit of God walking WITH man, but the upper room was the fruit of God walking IN man. In 2 Corinthians 6:16, God says, "I will dwell with them and walk in them. I will be their God, and they shall be My people."

The purest and most intimate language that we can speak to God with, is our unknown languages. We have unknown languages because they are otherworldly languages. When we speak in Tongues, it is just as supernatural as casting out devils, healing the sick and raising the dead. Many times, we are always asking how many souls got saved, how many devils have been cast out, or how many sick people got healed, or how many people were raised from the dead, which are all legit things to ask, but we also need to include asking, how much time have we put into praying in Tongues. We must realize that praying in Tongues will open up portals for the believer, to have all of these other supernatural manifestations listed above, consistent in our lives.

Isaiah 28:11 NIV

With foreign lips and strange tongues God will speak to this people

Isaiah 28:11 CEV

The Lord will speak to His people in strange sounds and foreign languages

Strange Tongues will produce strange things. Strange things is the word *paradoxos* in Greek where we get the word paradox from, which means something that contradicts. Tongues will produce things in your life from another world that will be contradictory to human intellect and the human way of reasoning. This word also means it opposes common sense. Tongues help to grow us into dimensions where God's ways and thoughts become our common sense, which also means that Tongues help us to exercise our spiritual senses. The word paradox also means uncommon, unexpected, remarkable things and extraordinary. Tongues help to produce an uncommon lifestyle. They help pull into our world remarkable and unexpected things and also influence us into an extraordinary perspective that causes us to live extraordinarily.

Unknown Tongues or otherworldly languages are our native languages because we are citizens of Heaven. Every citizen has a native language.

1 Cor. 14:2 GNT

Those who speak in strange tongues do not speak to others but to God, because no one understands them

TONGUES: LANGUAGES OF THE GOD CLASS

Otherworldly languages are foreign to this dimension, but they are citizenship languages in the world of God. These languages are non-comprehensible to this world.

Tongues are the languages of the light dimension. Just as darkness cannot comprehend light, Tongues are not comprehended by those that still walk in darkness. This is one of the reasons that demons cannot understand the coded messages spoken by Tongues. This is also one of the reasons that demons divide the church with doctrines that oppose speaking in Tongues. If we really think about it, whatever the devil decides to divide the church about, with different doctrines, we need to really do some digging into and ask ourselves, why is there so much division surrounding this certain topic. We need to keep an open ear to the realm of revelation about the divisions.

Our intellect was infected by darkness, this is why our state of thinking is in a delay compared to how the world of God thinks. This is why we always need revelation, because revelations are flashes of light-filled information that speed our thought processes back into original order. Yet then, since our thought processes were delayed by darkness, our intellect does not have the capacity to grasp the nature, the significance nor the meaning of God's otherworldly languages for all believers. It is very hard to value what we cannot comprehend.

When we pray, there is a release of energy that breaks through low dimensional distractions. Prayer has a tangible effect on it. I have experienced on many occasions that I have more natural energy, coming from the supernatural world and I am willing to do more natural responsibilities when my spirit man is strong. When Jesus filled us with the fullness of His Spirit, He filled us with New Wine. He started off with the Best Wine for the Last Days.

One of the main reasons why New Wine is so great, because wine gets better as it ages, and the New Wine of the Spirit is Ancient Wine. This Wine remains and stays consistent as the Best Wine. I do not drink natural alcohol, but I do have a lifestyle of praying in Tongues and I get drunk in another dimension. The posture of spending time praying in Tongues will push us into realms of drunkenness WITHOUT hangovers, headaches, and health problems. This type of drunkenness will IMPROVE our health.

Tongues or otherworldly languages are not for mere humans, but Tongues are for divine beings. Since we are citizens of Heaven that speak in our native Tongues, Tongues are foreign languages in the earth or extraterrestrial languages, which means that these languages originated outside of the earth.

Christ is the Mystic Secret of the Godhead. According to Ephesians 1:21, "Christ has been ascended and seated far above all principalities, powers, mights, and dominions," and everything else that can be named in the spirit world and the natural world. Mysteries are ascended information in the location of Christ and these secrets are above any being that has been created. As beings of the God class, we have divine access into these divine secrets that are able to be transferred into our spirit man from the location of Christ through the technology of Tongues.

We must realize that not only can Tongues be used for prayer in the spirit unto the Lord, but Tongues can also be used for worship in the spirit unto the Lord.

1 Corinthians 14:15 NKJV

[15] What is the conclusion then? I will pray with the spirit, and I will also pray with the understanding. I will sing with the spirit, and I will also sing with the understanding. We can also release the blessings of the Lord over others in the spirit, over your food, and etc., by praying in tongues

1 Corinthians 14:16-17 NKJV

[16] Otherwise, if you bless with the spirit, how will he who occupies the place of the uninformed say "Amen" at your giving of thanks, since he does not understand what you say? [17] For you indeed give thanks well, but the other is not edified.

1 Corinthians 14:18 NKJV

I thank my God I speak with tongues more than you all-

The word *more* is the Greek word *mallon*, which means in greater degrees, in greater depths and in greater dimensions. This also means that Paul proclaimed, I pray in greater degrees, greater depths and in greater dimensions of Tongues than all of you. Tongues usher us into different locations. Tongues have different locations in the spirit world, and they can locate what is on the earth. There is an increase that comes **TO** our tongue life, which navigates us into those greater dimensions and different locations. There is also an increase that comes **FROM** our tongue life. The more we pray in Tongues, the more locations we can explore and discover.

We obtain the benefit of the location, depending on the location that we travel into. Locations are not determined by the one speaking in Tongues, but locations are determined by the One that gives us the utterance. The Holy Spirit is the One that gives us the utterance. There are unlimited locations that our tongues can travel into, through the guidance and utterances of the Holy Spirit. My assignment is to give you a few locations in this book

Location of Mysteries

If we lack mysteries, we live predictable; we are mystical beings that are coming into more and more of a revealing knowledge of Christ.

1 Corinthians 14:2 NKJV

2 For he who speaks in a tongue does not speak to men but to God, for no one understands him; however, in the spirit he speaks mysteries.

TONGUES: LANGUAGES OF THE GOD CLASS

We have been baptized into the mystical body of Christ by the Mystic Secret of the Godhead. Now, we can speak out mysteries because Tongues are mystical languages. When we speak in Tongues, we speak mysteries from our spirits, and we speak forth into this realm the mysteries that are housed in the spirit realm. Tongues help to usher us into the BE NOT realm, speaking those things that BE NOT as though they BE.

If the Lord allowed mere, fallen men to understand Tongues, then men could corrupt this line of communication with their vain imaginations. The Lord wants to download into us His imaginations, His dreams, His thoughts and His desires through the channel of Tongues. He wanted us to have a pure channel of prayer, to pray out His will in the earth.

Mysteries in Greek are called *Musterion*. Mysteries are guarded revelations. They are what can only be known by way of revelation. If God does not reveal it, then it will remain a mystery to us. It will remain divine, secret things that are not obvious to our understanding.

Mysteries are otherworldly information. In order to understand these mysteries, you have to be otherworldly. Mysteries are for your pursuit so that your questions can be answered through the revelation of another realm. Mysteries are classified information or classified intelligence that are reserved for beings of a certain class.

When we steward mysteries, we can shift our personal economies. Our personal economies can shift by way of one revelation being downloaded into our spirit man. It is not about how much more work we can add to our life, because many of us are one revelation from God, away from living in a different and upgraded tax bracket. Mysteries are things in the spirit realm that are hidden, locked up, gated, coded, closed, sealed and fortified. These things are hidden FOR us not FROM us. These mysteries are equivalent to mighty things in Jeremiah.

Jeremiah 33:3 NKJV

3 'Call to Me, and I will answer you, and show you great and [b]mighty things, which you do not know.'

"Mighty things" in Hebrew are the word *batsar* and *yatsar* which means things that are cut off, unattainable, inaccessible, closed off, surrounded, gated and fortified. Light reveals, unveils, uncovers and exposes those things which are hidden. Tongues are languages of the light so Tongues will become the in-between portal that helps to reveal, unveil, expose and uncover what has been gated, closed off, fortified, surrounded, inaccessible and unattainable in the realm of God.

Mysteries also help us to locate depths that are in the word. They take us beyond shallow learning. When we take the time to pray out of the realm of mysteries, we will access help for us that redeems the time. The mystery realm is also the realm where the knowledge of the glory is revealed.

2 Corinthians 4:6 NKJV

6 For it is the God who commanded light to shine out of darkness, who has shone in our hearts to give the light of the knowledge of the glory of God in the face of Jesus Christ.

The Holy Spirit is our Face-to-face Intimate partner. He is the One that reveals Jesus to us. Therefore, the knowledge of the glory is the Face of Jesus. Accordingly, when the Holy Spirit reveals unto us new dimensions of His glory, He is revealing new dimensions of the image of Christ. Moses was a shadow and type of this dimension. The glory in the law of Moses gave life to Moses and he saw the law as a reflection of a relationship. Moses lived 120 years on a glory that was in the law. It was a glory that faded but it was also a glory that shined and gave life.

In the upper room, the Lord broke us into a new legacy and a new glory. The glory of sonship which is a Face-to-face glory. It is a Spirit-to-spirit glory and a never ending glory. When we remain in the realm of mystery, everything concerning the life of God for us starts to unfold. We see the unfolding of the life of God in Paul's life as well. Paul remained in the realm of mysteries because he stayed saturated in Tongues.

Musterion in Greek also means the operation of hidden angelic forces that will accelerate the kingdom of Heaven in our lives. This is the place where hidden angels assist us and make the kingdom of Heaven a reality to us. This brings me to my next location.

The Location of Angels

1 Corinthians 13:1 NKJV

Though I speak with the tongues of men and of angels, but have not love, I have become sounding brass or a clanging cymbal.

Paul speaks of speaking in the Tongues of angels. That means that God gives us the utterance of angelic Tongues. In this location, angels will become messengers to us through angelic languages. In fact, praying in this location will increase angelic activity around us. Also, not only is God attracted to the languages of the spirit, but so are angels. The languages of the spirit strengthens the presence of the angelic realm among us.

For example, one day I was in Florida at my good friend's church, Apostle Chazdon Strickland. We were in a meeting with some of his leaders and we gathered to pray, and we all started praying in Tongues together. While we were praying in Tongues, I started sensing the room shift and I said to myself, "We are in the location of angels" and as soon as I said that to myself, Apostle Chazdon said over the mic, "This is the dimension of angels and angels are in the room". The angelic activity in the room became very high. We were sensitive to their presence. I understood the Tongues of angels in operation at that moment, in a corporate setting.

TONGUES: LANGUAGES OF THE GOD CLASS

In this location, angels come to encounter us and assist us in ministry. Ministering angels are highly active in administrating the affairs of Heaven into the Earth in this location. When angels come to speak to us, since they are spirits, they come to speak to our spirit man. They are speaking to our spirit man in THEIR languages and because our spirit man knows their language, our spirit man can interpret or understand what they are saying as if it was our earthly language.

I also believe that this is the dimension where the corporate believers came together and gave themselves over to the intercession of the Holy Spirit and Peter was freed from prison by way of angelic assistance. Angels protect us when we pray in tongues. The Tongues of men and the Tongues of angels are both Tongues for ministering to others. However, neither the tongues of men nor the Tongues of angels are the Tongues that keep us in the love of God as Jude describes. The only tongues that keep us in intimacy with God and keep us in the love of God are the Tongues that personally edify us. These are the unknown languages that talk directly to God and He alone understands.

Angels are heavily involved in spiritual warfare. They are protectors. They are beings that fight on our behalf. There are countless testimonies from people like me and others who have been protected by angels while they were speaking in Tongues. I personally have been protected from accidents, major storms, and dangers aware and unaware while praying in the languages of God. I remember hearing a testimony about two women that were being abducted by a taxi driver who threatened to rape and kill them. When the young women got in the taxi, the taxi driver started driving off and locked the young ladies in the back seat. He told them what he planned to do to them and the young ladies immediately started speaking in Tongues. All of a sudden, the taxi driver saw angels running on both sides of the car. He stopped the vehicle, got out, and ran off! The young ladies were saved by angels that manifested in the natural realm because of their prayers. Instead of the young ladies allowing fear to control them and submitting themselves to the abduction and threats of this demonized taxi driver, they used their supernatural weapon called Tongues and the unseen realm showed up on their behalf to protect them.

Location of Wisdom

Since Tongues are the languages of God, it also means that they are languages from above. This also means that praying in the languages of God will not just unlock mysteries from above but also wisdom from above.

James 3:17 NKJV

17 But the wisdom that is from above is first pure, then peaceable, gentle, willing to yield, full of mercy and good fruits, without partiality and without hypocrisy.

72

Wisdom is a skillful application that comes from the intelligence of the mind. This type of intelligence is from above, which means it is an intelligence that we do not have any knowledge of. Also, this wisdom is above the mind of man, the mind of the earth, the mind of what is sensual and the mind of the demonic.

Descended wisdom is the application of intelligence that comes from the mind of man, the mind of carnality, the mind of what is sensual or unspiritual, and a demonic mind. It is lower dimension wisdom. James describes the character or the fruit of the wisdom that manifests from above: purity, being peaceable, being gentle, yielding, full of mercy, full of good fruits, impartial, and without hypocrisy. The opposite of all of these are characteristics of descended wisdom: impurity, chaotic, harsh, unyielding, merciless, bad fruits, partiality, hypocritical.

1 Corinthians 2:6-8 NKJV

6 However, we speak wisdom among those who are mature, yet not the wisdom of this age, nor of the rulers of this age, who are coming to nothing. 7 But we speak the wisdom of God in a mystery, the hidden wisdom which God [c]ordained before the ages for our glory, 8 which none of the rulers of this age knew; for had they known, they would not have crucified the Lord of glory.

Hidden wisdom is wisdom that is concealed or classified. Jesus's death was Classified Wisdom. Wisdom that the god of this age nor his rulers that were serving him as agents, had revelation of. This wisdom was too far above their knowledge to even comprehend. Satan was the first one to manifest ignorance from his heavenly identity as Lucifer, the son of the morning and custodian of light. His fall into satan reidentified him as the fallen one and adversary. However, even ignorance is still intelligence and a wisdom. It is an intelligence and a wisdom that is not from above. It is lower than the intelligence and wisdom that comes from God. Satan can blind the minds of others because he was the first one that became blind. He became blind by descending from the knowledge of God.

This is why the plan of the Father was able to be executed effectively without being hindered by Satan. Things were hidden from him and his agents because the Father's plan was an intelligence that required a higher way of thinking and operating. Jesus died as Legal Wisdom from ABOVE. This is why the Cross is FOOLISHNESS to those that are perishing. When people are perishing, that means that they are in a location that is outside of the location of God. They are not in the IN HIM location. The Cross is not just foolishness to human beings that are perishing but also spirit beings that are perishing.

Even though the devil is full of wisdom, the wisdom from above is still classified information to him. It is above his pay grade, so to speak. The crucifixion was classified information. It was wisdom guarded from those that are not in God's location. This is also one of the reasons that our weapons of warfare are from the intelligence of classified information revealed and not the intelligence of carnality. Carnality is descended information that has become common to ordinary and fallen beings. We must learn how to set our minds on wisdom that is from the dimensions of above and not on the wisdom of man.

Location of Faith

Tongues do not give us faith, but Tongues will help to increase, build up, energize and activate the faith that we already possess. Jude 1:20 says "to pray in the spirit and build up your most holy faith". He gave us a technology that will help us to bypass all unbelief through Tongues. All of the supernatural world was meant to be understood through faith and by revelation. Faith is the operational system for all the trading systems and business transactions between Heaven and Earth and between the supernatural world and the natural world. Faith is rooted in intelligence. Faith is built up when we gain intelligence about the realm of the unseen. In fact, the more intelligent that we become about the unseen world, that intelligence increases our faith in possessing what we see.

Faith makes the possibilities of God a reality to us. Impossibilities are not even in the vocabulary of those that are full of faith. When we do not live from the realm of faith, by default, we automatically live by sight. Sight is the dimension where we become more sensitive to the senses of the natural body which involves the realm of carnality. This is the sensual realm. It is the realm of the natural five senses which are descended senses.

Remember, praying in the spirit keeps us in the realm of faith and in the realm of the supernatural. Also, praying in the spirit keeps us from fulfilling the desires of our flesh. Faith breaks our connection to being shaped by the world.

Location of Divine Health

1 Corinthians 14:4

He who speaks in a tongue edifies himself

The word *edifies* means to build or repair the house. What house? The house that houses your spirit man which is your physical body. Also, it means to build himself up or in other words, to improve himself. It is a means of restoration, repair, and rebuilding. It is to literally HEAL himself. Tongues are a limitless self-improvement mechanism.

Tongues are gateway languages that help to repair our bodies and our minds on a cellular level. In fact, Tongues will also boost our immune system. The majority of sicknesses, ailments and illnesses that we experience in our bodies are caused by pressures, worries, fears, cares and torments. The supernatural languages of God will help bring rejuvenation to our bodies. A study done by the American Journal of Human Biology found that speaking in Tongues is associated with both a reduction in circulatory cortisol, and enhancements in alpha-amylase enzyme activity – two common biomarkers of stress reduction that can be measured in saliva. According to the New York Times article, a study of nearly 1,000 Evangelical Christians in England found that those engaged in the practice of speaking in Tongues were more emotionally stable than those who did not. Contrary to what may be a common perception, studies suggest that people who speak in Tongues rarely suffer from mental problems. Additionally, a few years ago, a brain surgeon at Oral Roberts University did a study of what happens in the brain when people pray in Tongues. He found that they secreted two chemicals that can boost the immune system by 35-40%!

Acts 28:1-6 NKJV

Now when they had escaped, they then found out that the island was called Malta. 2 And the natives[a] showed us unusual kindness; for they kindled a fire and made us all welcome, because of the rain that was falling and because of the cold. 3 But when Paul had gathered a bundle of sticks and laid them on the fire, a viper came out because of the heat, and fastened on his hand. 4 So when the natives saw the creature hanging from his hand, they said to one another, "No doubt this man is a murderer, whom, though he has escaped the sea, yet justice does not allow to live." 5 But he shook off the creature into the fire and suffered no harm. 6 However, they were expecting that he would swell up or suddenly fall down dead. But after they had looked for a long time and saw no harm come to him, they changed their minds and said that he was a god.

It was a mystery to the people concerning why Paul did not die from the venom of the viper. What they did not know was, Paul had already prayed out the mysteries in Tongues concerning divine health and divine life that invaded his natural body. Paul was full of life. The venom became of non-effect because in that moment, Paul's body carried resurrection power. Supernaturally, life swallowed death in that moment. Paul did not die but the venom died, and death died in that moment.

Location of Intercession

There will always be prayer barriers when we pray in our understanding. Our prayer strength and our prayer jurisdictions will always become predicated upon our spheres of revelation. Wherever revelation is limited, our prayer lives will become limited. Also, praying in the languages of God will remove prayer barriers because they help to lengthen and enlarge the parameters of our revelation. The languages of the Spirit will bring us breakthroughs in the areas of our prayer weaknesses and prayer inadequacies.

Romans 8:26-27 NKJV

6 Likewise the Spirit also helps in our weaknesses. For we do not know what we should pray for as we ought, but the Spirit Himself makes intercession [g]for us with groanings which cannot be uttered. 27 Now He who searches the hearts knows what the mind of the Spirit is, because He makes intercession for the saints according to the will of God.

The word *helps* here also means that He *joins to help* or, in other words, take hold together with us against something. The Holy Spirit is literally our HELP! Furthermore, the word *weaknesses* point to our infirmities which are the inability to produce results. This is prayer shortcomings, prayer weaknesses, and even shortcomings and weaknesses in life. Paul then mentions groanings that cannot be uttered. These are sounds that cannot be pronounced with articulate speech. Basically, things that will not be understood in this dimension.

The Holy Spirit will release through us sounds that will not be understood in this dimension, but these same prayer sounds will help us pray into things that we have the inability to pray in our own understanding. Remember, there are depths of prayer that can only be attained by speaking in the languages of God. Tongues will help us build rank in our prayer life.

Ephesians 6:18 NKJV

*18 praying always with all prayer and supplication **in the Spirit**, being watchful to this end with all perseverance and supplication for all the saints—*

Location of Worship

John 4:24 NKJV

24 God is Spirit, and those who worship Him must worship in spirit and truth. "

Notice, worshiping in Tongues help us to locate God in worship, when our understanding fails to locate Him. We need to sing with our understanding but many times our understanding doesn't always locate the pulse of His heart.

1 Corinthians 14:15 NKJV

15 What is the conclusion then? I will pray with the spirit, and I will also pray with the understanding. I will sing with the spirit, and I will also sing with the understanding.

Tongues can take us into worship without us focusing on what to say in our understanding. As a matter of fact, after certain periods of tongue worship, the words of understanding from Heaven start to drop into our spirit understanding and then our spirit understanding channels it into our mental understanding and then we sing what we hear.

Tongues can help take us into dimensions of birthing out fresh psalms, hymns, spiritual songs and melodies in the spirit from our spirits unto the Lord.

Ephesians 5:19 NKJV

19 speaking to one another in psalms and hymns and spiritual songs, singing and making melody in your heart to the Lord,

Location of the Prophetic Dimension

Tongues are very prophetic in nature. It is in the understanding and the interpretation of Tongues that we access the ability to edify others. Tongues are the stirring embers into the prophetic dimension.

1 Corinthians 14:4-5 NKJV

4 He who speaks in a tongue edifies himself, but he who prophesies edifies the church. 5 I wish you all spoke with tongues, but even more that you prophesied; [a]for he who prophesies is greater than he who speaks with tongues, unless indeed he interprets, that the church may receive edification.

TONGUES: LANGUAGES OF THE GOD CLASS

Paul compares Tongues to the prophetic in a corporate setting. In a corporate setting, the prophetic trumps Tongues. Why? It is because of understanding. The prophetic does not trump Tongues in the spirit world, it trumps Tongues in the world of comprehension when we have to teach, edify and minister to the church. For the church must be able to understand or comprehend what you are ministering to them by way of the Holy Spirit.

Tongues bypass your understanding and the prophetic speaks to your understanding. Tongues shut down the lower part of you, so that the higher part of you can communicate with the world that it is connected to. There are Tongues given to all believers and then there are Tongues appointed to certain believers in the church for the ministry to the church.

1 Corinthians 12:28-31 NKJV

*28 And God has appointed these in the church: first apostles, second prophets, third teachers, after that miracles, then gifts of healings, helps, administrations, **varieties of tongues**. 29 Are all apostles? Are all prophets? Are all teachers? Are all workers of miracles? 30 Do all have gifts of healings? **Do all speak with tongues? Do all interpret**? 31 But earnestly desire the [i]best gifts. And yet I show you a more excellent way.*

Also notice that those that operate in the ministries of the word have rank over those that just minister in the gifts.

Remember, the ministry of the Word takes precedence over the gifts because the Word is the final authority. Attention is drawn when the question is asked, do all speak with Tongues? In this context, this is talking about the ministry gift of Tongues, not the Tongues that are given to all believers by way of the baptism of the Holy Spirit. The ministry gift of Tongues is not given to all believers, but the Tongues that come with being baptized in the Holy Spirit are accessible to and is for ALL BELIEVERS.

In Conclusion, Tongues, are ancient tools from the Lord that give us access to the building of our faith and they have become a source of power, guidance, and wisdom. Tongues open the doors of access to the Dimensions of God and locations of divine mysteries so that we can administrate and reveal the Will of God in the earth. We as New Creation sons are charged with establishing God's Dominion and bringing His Kingdom into the earth as it is in Heaven. Tongues, the Languages of God, are supernatural tools that help us to become fully equipped and able to accomplish God's purpose in sending us to the planet.

ISBN: 979-8-218-63186-4

www.ingramcontent.com/pod-product-compliance
Lightning Source LLC
Chambersburg PA
CBHW061710120626
46550CB00003B/1166